Contents

Any words appearing in the text in bold, **like this**, are explained in the glossary.

REGIONS OF THE WORLD

South Asia

Mark Stewart

Heinemann
LIBRARY

www.heinemann.co.uk/library
Visit our website to find out more information about Heinemann Library books.

To order:
☎ Phone 44 (0) 1865 888112
▤ Send a fax to 44 (0) 1865 314091
▣ Visit the Heinemann bookshop at www.heinemann.co.uk/library to browse our catalogue and order online.

First published in Great Britain by Heinemann Library, Halley Court, Jordan Hill, Oxford OX2 8EJ, part of Harcourt Education.
Heinemann is a registered trademark of Harcourt Education Ltd.

© Harcourt Education Ltd 2008
First published in paperback in 2009
The moral right of the proprietor has been asserted.

Editorial: Andrew Farrow
Design: Steve Mead and Q2A Creative
Illustrations: International Mapping Associates, Inc
Picture Research: Melissa Allison
Production: Alison Parsons

Originated by Chroma Graphics (Overseas) Pte.
Printed and bound in China by Leo Paper Group

ISBN 978 0 431 90715 4 (hardback)
12 11 10 09 08
10 9 8 7 6 5 4 3 2 1

ISBN 978 0 431 90724 6 (paperback)
13 12 11 10 09
10 9 8 7 6 5 4 3 2 1

British Library Cataloguing in Publication Data
Stewart, Mark
South Asia. - (Regions of the world)   1.
South Asia - Geography - Juvenile literature
I. Title
915.4

A full catalogue record for this book is available from the British Library.

Acknowledgments
The author and publishers are grateful to the following for permission to reproduce copyrighted material:

© Alamy (Danita Delimont) **35** (Images&Stories) **45** (Jochen Tack) **42** (Mike Goldwater) **46** (Neil McAllister) **25** (Robert Harding Picture Library) **30**; © FLPA/Reinard Dirschell **13**; © Getty Images (Keystone) **9** (AFP Photo/ Aamir Qureshi) **55**; © Lonely Planet Images/Richard I'Anson **27**; © Mountain Camera Picture Library/John Cleare **10**; © PA Photos (AP/Geert Vanden Wijngaert) **28** (AP/Tomas Munita) **33**; © Panos Pictures (Chris Stowers) **17** (Mark Henley) **19, 44, 49** (Martin Adler) **29**; © Robert Harding (Travel Library) **22** (Doug Traverso) **41** (Jane Sweeney) **20** (John Wilson) **4** (Marco Simoni) **36** bottom; © Science Photo Library/NASA **21**; © Still Pictures (Jorgen Schytte) **40** (Joerg Boethling) **51, 53** (José Giribás) **47** (Mark Edwards) **39** (ullstein – Hartmann) **32** (ullstein – Hechtenberg) **36** top (ullstein – Hechtenberg) **50**.

Cover photograph of an Indian dancer reproduced with permission of TIPS Images/ Pietro Scozzari

The publishers would like to thank Daniel Block for his assistance in the preparation of this book.

Every effort has been made to contact copyright holders of any material reproduced in this book. Any omissions will be rectified in subsequent printings if notice is given to the publishers.

Disclaimer
All the Internet addresses (URLs) given in this book were valid at the time of going to press. However, due to the dynamic nature of the Internet, some addresses may have changed, or sites may have changed or ce_____
pu_____
re_____
ac_____

Introducing South Asia

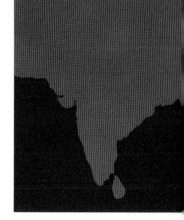

The Asian continent is the largest on Earth. The region of South Asia, which includes eight countries (Afghanistan, Bangladesh, Bhutan, India, Maldives, Nepal, Pakistan, and Sri Lanka), makes up about 15 percent of this landmass and contains about a third of its people. The largest country in the region is India. This part of the world is sometimes called the Indian subcontinent because India and its neighbours sit on a continental plate that collided with the rest of Asia millions of years ago.

The geography of South Asia varies greatly. The region includes the world's tallest mountains and some of its most powerful rivers. It covers barren **deserts**, fertile plains, and fantastic tropical islands. The people of South Asia feel a deep connection to the natural world. The natural world forms the basis for much of their culture and many of their religious beliefs, and provides them with the resources they need to live.

The most precious resource in South Asia, as in all places, is water. Without it, the region's 1.5 billion people would not have the food, drinking water, or power they need to survive. Most people in South Asia live close to water sources. Those who do not have found clever ways to survive on very little. Indeed, the history of South Asia is the story of humankind's ability to survive and thrive in a stunning range of environments. From ancient times to today, the relationship between the people and the land has determined the course of events in this region.

← Another day dawns for the people of South Asia. Here, the Sun rises over the Ganges River at Varanasi, India.

The cities of South Asia

Approximately one-fifth of the world's population lives in the eight nations that make up South Asia. The most heavily populated country is India, which has about 1.1 billion people, followed by Pakistan (165 million), Bangladesh (150 million), Afghanistan (32 million), Nepal (29 million), Sri Lanka (21 million), Bhutan (2.3 million), and Maldives (369,000). The great majority of the 1.5 billion people in South Asia live in small towns and villages, some of which are located in extremely rugged or desolate areas. The standard of living in much of the region is extremely low, so a great deal of time and effort is devoted to basic day-to-day survival.

However, South Asia is also a region of huge cities. The number of people living in urban environments is about 250 million, which is almost equal to the population of the entire United States. There are five **metropolitan areas** in South Asia with populations of 10 million or more. They are New Delhi, Mumbai, and Kolkata (all in India), Karachi (Pakistan), and Dhaka (Bangladesh). By comparison the only European cities with metropolitan areas of more than 10 million are London and Paris. In the United States, only New York City and Los Angeles have populations of more than 10 million. Many other urban centres in South Asia have more than a million residents.

Moving

People who move into cities usually do so to find better employment and education opportunities. Advances in food production, health, science, communications, and **commerce** have made it possible for many millions of people to live close together in South Asia's cities, which have grown very rapidly in just one or two generations as a result. Despite these advances, overpopulation and the poverty it brings is still the biggest challenge for the region.

NAME CHANGE

In recent years, many Indian cities have altered their names to more traditional pronunciations and spellings. Cities such as Bombay, Bangalore, and Calcutta (names originally bestowed by their Portuguese and British **colonial** rulers) have changed to Mumbai, Bengaluru, and Kolkata, respectively. The city of Madras, the centre of India's car industry, was renamed Chennai. In most cases, the name change was meant to symbolize a break from the region's colonial past and to reaffirm India's hard-won independence.

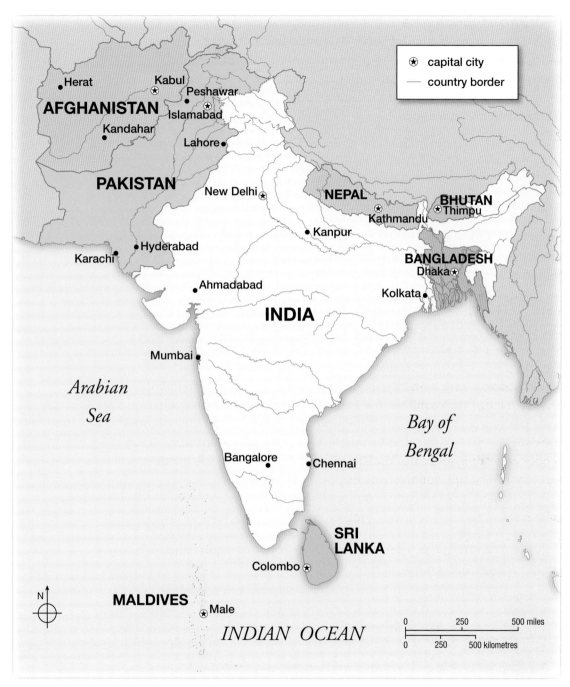

⊛	capital city
—	country border

• Herat

Kabul ⊛

Peshawar ⊛

AFGHANISTAN

Islamabad ⊛

• Kandahar

Lahore •

PAKISTAN

New Delhi ⊛

NEPAL

Kathmandu ⊛

BHUTAN

⊛ Thimpu

• Kanpur

• Hyderabad

Karachi •

BANGLADESH

Dhaka ⊛

• Ahmadabad

Kolkata •

INDIA

Mumbai •

Arabian Sea

Bay of Bengal

Bangalore • • Chennai

SRI LANKA

Colombo ⊛

N

MALDIVES ⊛ Male

INDIAN OCEAN

0	250	500 miles
0	250	500 kilometres

This political map shows the eight independent countries of South Asia. This is a region of both large cities and remote areas. All the countries and their statistics are listed on page 56.

History of South Asia

The first major civilization of South Asia emerged in the Indus River valley around 2500 BCE. A series of invading cultures, including the Greeks under Alexander the Great, ruled the area until the 10th century. At that time, much of present-day Afghanistan, Pakistan, and India became part of the **Islamic** Mogul Empire.

The Moguls swept down from the plains of Central Asia and defeated one army after another. They were excellent horsemen and archers. During the 17th century, their empire stretched across more than 4 million square kilometres (1.5 million square miles) of South Asia. At the time, the Mogul Empire was the largest in the world. The greatest Mogul ruler was Akbar. He welcomed new ideas and embraced the many cultures in his empire and beyond. This blending of art, literature, and religion can still be seen in the region today.

In the 19th century, Britain gained control of the region. The British favoured followers of **Hinduism**. During Britain's rule, the **Muslim** people of South Asia grew resentful of the **Hindus**, who gained economic and political influence from their close association with the British.

In 1947, after a long and difficult struggle, India won its independence. That same year, its mostly Muslim eastern and northwestern regions were partitioned into separate **dominions**, which would one day become the countries of Pakistan and Bangladesh. This division of territory along religious lines triggered a migration of people across the new borders.

The island of Ceylon (later renamed Sri Lanka) became a self-governing member of the Commonwealth of Nations in 1948. The Commonwealth of Nations was made up primarily of former British colonies that banded together after declaring their independence. Maldives, ruled by Islamic **sultans** for many centuries, became independent in 1965.

Although Afghanistan is not a rich or fertile country, it is one of history's most-invaded nations. That is because it sits at the crossroads of South Asia, Central Asia, and the Middle East. It gained independence from Britain in 1919.

The mountain kingdoms of Bhutan and Nepal were almost completely isolated from the rest of the world for much of their history. In 563 BCE, Prince Siddhartha Gautama, the founder of **Buddhism**, was born in the region that is known today as Nepal.

MAN OF PEACE

In the mid-20th century, Mohandas Gandhi (1869–1948) led India's fight for independence from Great Britain. He was known as the Mahatma, or 'Great Soul'. Gandhi believed that freedom could be won through **civil disobedience**, and he was right. The non-violent non-cooperation of millions of Indians convinced the British that continuing their rule over the country was useless. Gandhi was greatly influenced by the 19th-century American author Henry David Thoreau, who believed that refusing to obey certain laws was a form of respectful disagreement. Gandhi's ideas influenced later civil rights campaigners, such as the American civil rights leader Martin Luther King Jr. .

The strategy of non-violent non-cooperation preached by Mohandas Gandhi (centre) helped to win independence for India in 1947. Standing next to Gandhi are two of India's early leaders, Pandit Nehru (left) and Vallabhai Patel (right).

Natural features

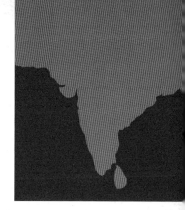

The great ethnic and religious diversity of South Asia, as well as the region's fascinating history, are a direct result of its widely varying geography. A journey by air from the western edge of Afghanistan to the eastern edge of India would cover more than 3,700 kilometres (2,300 miles). It would pass some of the driest, wettest, and tallest places on Earth. A trip from the towering K2 mountain in the Karakoram Range to the southern tip of Sri Lanka in the Indian Ocean would cover roughly the same distance. The journey would cover equally dramatic landforms, including the Great Indian Desert and the Deccan Plateau. More than 645 kilometres (400 miles) southwest of Sri Lanka is the beginning of the Maldives, a string of coral **atolls** covering more than 90,650 square kilometres (35,000 square miles).

Before the invention of the aeroplane, such journeys would have been possible only by land or sea. The dramatic physical characteristics of South Asia made travel difficult and dangerous. Steep mountains, wide deserts, and powerful rivers served to both protect and isolate regional populations. This enabled different cultures to evolve and flourish. These multiple cultures, with their different customs, economies, religious beliefs, styles of dress, and cuisines, have come together in countless ways over the centuries and can still be seen and experienced by travellers throughout the region.

← Annapurna is the name for a series of peaks in the Himalayas. Annapurna 1 (A1) is the tenth highest summit in the world. The name *Annapurna* means 'goddess of the harvests' in the Sanskrit language.

Major bodies of water

The major bodies of water surrounding South Asia are the Arabian Sea, Indian Ocean, and Bay of Bengal. The Indian Ocean is the third largest in the world. Its warm waters do not contain high levels of plankton, so commercial fishing is not always possible. However, the Indian Ocean has long been a key factor in South Asia's economic success. Millions of tonnes of goods flow in and out of the region's major ports each year.

The ocean is the source of the **monsoons** that bring vital rainfall to Pakistan, India, and Bangladesh. The monsoon changes direction with the seasons, carrying moisture up from the southwest each summer. When the land is at its hottest, it creates a **low-pressure system** that draws the monsoon winds up from the Indian Ocean and Arabian Sea. As winter approaches and the land is cooler, the warmer air over the sea rises, and the monsoon winds reverse direction and blow out to sea.

The western coast of South Asia is on the Arabian Sea. The Arabian Sea has provided a trade connection between India, Africa, and the Middle East for many centuries. Today, it is a part of the shipping route from India to Europe, through Egypt's Suez Canal. The triangular-shaped Bay of Bengal forms the northeastern tip of the Indian Ocean and is the end point for several of the region's major rivers. The beautiful sands of Cox's Bazar, located near Chittagong, Bangladesh, are part of the world's longest natural sea beach.

TSUNAMI

On 26 December 2004, an earthquake under the Indian Ocean produced an enormous surge of water called a tsunami. It crashed into the coastline of Sri Lanka and India, killing more than 50,000 people in these countries. Had a warning system been in place among the nations that surround the Indian Ocean, there would have been time to evacuate many coastal towns. Work has now begun to create a warning system, which scientists hope will save lives when future undersea earthquakes occur. Meanwhile, simpler measures are being taken across the region. Although many seaside villages were wiped out, a few, such the Indian town of Naluvedapathy, survived thanks to thick groves of coconut palms planted at the water's edge. People in many villages are now planting trees as an inexpensive and effective way to protect themselves in the future.

The lionfish, or turkeyfish, is one of the many unusual species that can be found in the coral reefs and other shallow waters of the eastern Indian Ocean.

Rivers

The rivers of South Asia are like the arteries of the human body. They bring water for drinking, transport, irrigation, and power to a billion people in the region. The major rivers also deposit mineral-rich silt to agricultural areas. Silt is created by the weathering of rocks in the mountains and is different from sand and clay. It contains nutrients that are light enough to be carried thousands of miles. The buildup of silt in the **deltas** where rivers empty into the sea makes these areas rich in plant and animal life.

THE GANGES DOLPHIN

One of the rarest and most beautiful animals in the world is the Ganges dolphin. The dolphin lives only in fresh water and is named after the river in India in which it is most often found. At 1.5–2.5 metres (5–8 feet) long, it is larger than most saltwater dolphins. It also has very poor eyesight. The dolphin swims and catches food using echolocation, emitting clicks and calls into the surrounding environment and then 'reading' the echoes that bounce back. The Ganges dolphin can swim on its side, stirring up the riverbed in its search for food.

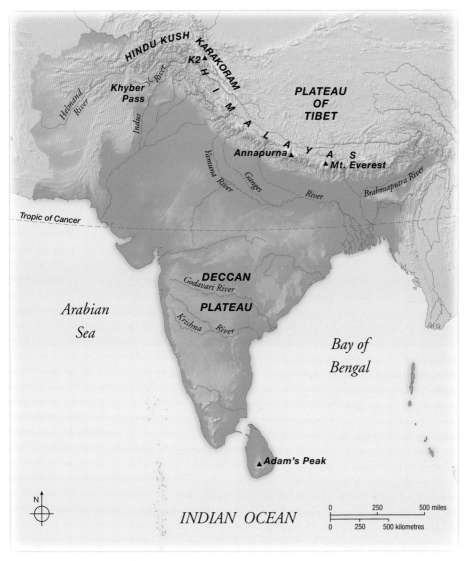

With its vast plateaus and the tallest mountains in the world, South Asia is an area of many contrasts.

Without these silt deposits, the fields of South Asia would be unable to produce enough crops, and countless people would starve. The three most important rivers are the Indus, Ganges, and Brahmaputra. Others include the Amu Darya, Godavari, Krishna, and Helmand. Each is fed by the mountains that form the northern border of the region.

Sacred waters

To Hindus, the Ganges (or Ganga) is not just a river, it is a goddess. Hindus believe that bathing in the river at certain times is a way to erase sin and achieve salvation. Water from the Ganges is considered holy water, and many Hindus around the world keep a small bottle of water from the river in their homes. Many Hindu festivals are held along the banks of the Ganges. Pollution is currently a serious threat to the Ganges, and India's government is working on ways to protect the river for future generations.

The Ganges begins high in the Himalayas in northern India. Many smaller rivers feed into the river as it flows southeast through the fertile Ganges Plain into Bangladesh. There it connects with the Brahmaputra River near the capital city of Dhaka and empties into the Bay of Bengal, about 2,510 kilometres (1,560 miles) from where it began. The Ganges Delta, sometimes called the Bengal Delta, is the largest in the world, covering almost 77,700 square kilometres (30,000 square miles).

The Indus River begins in the mountains of Tibet. It flows through the Kashmir region and then through Pakistan, where it joins with six other rivers before flowing into the Arabian Sea, southeast of the port city of Karachi. The Indus is nearly 3,200 kilometres (2,000 miles) long and feeds Pakistan's chief agricultural regions in the Punjab and Sindh provinces. Unlike most river deltas, the Indus Delta contains mostly infertile, clay-like soil. Although little grows in this swampy area, it is an important stop for hundreds of species of migrating birds. The Indus, along with the Brahmaputra, is one of a small number of rivers in the world that are subjected to the tides of the surrounding sea.

The long, slow-flowing Brahmaputra is an important transport waterway. The Brahmaputra begins in Tibet and rushes into South Asia through dramatic mountain gorges in the Himalayas. It flows gently southwest through India's Assam Valley and then turns south into Bangladesh, where it is known as the Jamuna. The name Brahmaputra means 'son of Brahma' in Sanskrit. Brahma is the Hindu god of creation. The name is unusual for the region because most rivers in India have female names.

REACH FOR THE SKY

The rocks that form the Himalayas were once under water. About 40 million years ago, the Indian landmass drifted north and collided with the Eurasian landmass. The collision pushed rock up from the sea bed to form the world's tallest mountains. Fossilized sea creatures have been found in the rock on many Himalayan peaks.

Mountains

The dividing line between the countries of South Asia and China is a collar of mountains formed by the Hindu Kush and Karakoram Ranges, and the Himalayas. The Himalayas are the highest mountains in the world, towering over India, Nepal, and Bhutan. The range includes Everest and Annapurna, two of the most spectacular peaks on the planet. The water from the Himalayas supplies India with its life-giving river system.

Though not as well-known as many of the world's other mountain ranges, the rugged, **arid** Hindu Kush are among the highest peaks in the world. They run through eastern Afghanistan from Tajikistan and China to the country's border with Pakistan. The Karakoram Range divides India, Pakistan, and China. The range's most famous peak is K2, which soars 8,611 metres (28,251 feet) above sea level.

Troubled peaks

The mountains of South Asia are known mostly for their awesome beauty. The mountainous Kashmir region that lies between India and Pakistan is famous as the home of the goats that produce cashmere wool. It is also part of the habitat of the endangered snow leopard. Unfortunately, Kashmir is also known for violence and suffering. The region has been in dispute since the two countries became independent, and many people have died in the battle for control. In 2005 a magnitude 7.6 earthquake struck the region. Nearly 100,000 people lost their lives, and almost four million people were left homeless.

Earthquakes are a danger throughout South Asia, particularly in the mountainous regions. That is because the Indian subcontinent is still grinding its way north into Asia at a rate of about 50 milimetres (2 inches) every year. Great pressure builds up and is suddenly released, causing the ground to shake violently. Only the strongest buildings survive the earthquakes.

⬆ This used to be the central marketplace of the town of Balakot in northwest Pakistan. It was destroyed by the earthquake of October 2005.

ASCENDING EVEREST

At 8,849 metres (29,035 feet), Mount Everest, on the border of Nepal and China, is the world's highest mountain. Many people tried and failed to reach the peak of Everest during the 19th and 20th centuries. The first to accomplish this feat were climbing partners Edmund Hillary and Tenzing Norgay in 1953.

Improvements in techniques and technology over the next half-century enabled many more people to reach the top of Everest. By the end of 2006, more than 2,000 people had successfully reached its summit, though more than 200 had died trying. Today, lovers of the mountain complain of 'traffic jams' and rubbish scattered on the slopes. They point out that respecting Everest means more than climbing safely. It is up to climbers to preserve this wonder for future generations.

Water all around

South Asia has many islands, including two island nations, Sri Lanka and Maldives. Sri Lanka lies off the southeastern tip of India and is about 64,750 square kilometres (25,000 square miles). The country was called Ceylon until 1972; the name Sri Lanka means 'resplendent island' in the Sinhalese language. Sri Lanka has been home to **Buddhists** and Hindus for many centuries, and during that time there have been violent struggles for power. When Sri Lanka was hit by a tsunami in 2004, the two groups put their differences aside and worked together to help the people. Once the crisis was over, however, the two sides began fighting again.

The people of Sri Lanka have an excellent railway system that connects the island's major cities. They also have of one of the best educational systems in South Asia. Ninety-six percent of Sri Lankans are literate, by far the highest rate in the region. In comparison, India's literacy rate is just 60 percent.

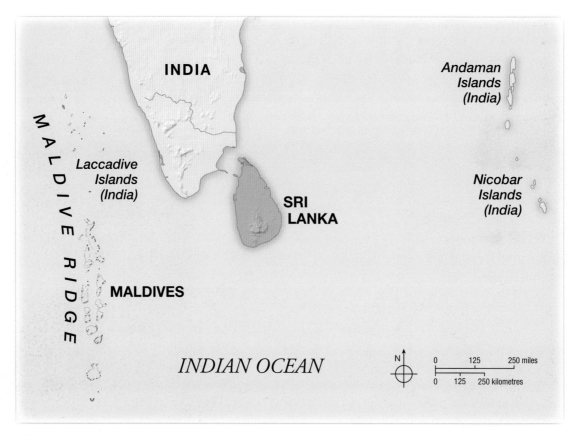

The island countries of South Asia have their own cultures, wildlife, and natural environments.

MADAME PRIME MINISTER

In 1960, Sri Lanka (then called Ceylon) made Sirimavo Bandaranaike the world's first female prime minister. She succeeded her husband, who had been assassinated in 1959. Women do not typically hold political or economic power in South Asian countries. However, women have occupied leadership roles in the region, including Indira Gandhi (India) and Benazir Bhutto (Pakistan).

The Republic of Maldives is a group of atolls in the Indian Ocean, located about 644 kilometres (400 miles) south and west of Sri Lanka. The country is made up of more than 1,000 islands, none of which rise more than 1.83 metres (6 feet) above sea level. Only about 200 of the islands are inhabited. As the Earth's temperature rises and sea ice melts into the oceans, people living in coastal cities worry about what the future holds. **Global warming** is a great concern to the Maldivian people, because rising oceans could actually make their country uninhabitable.

Other islands in South Asia include three groups that belong to India – the Nicobars and Andamans in the Bay of Bengal, and the Laccadives in the Arabian Sea. Many unique species of birds and animals live on these islands.

A public ferry crowded with passengers arrives at Fort Cochin in Kerala, India. Ferries are a popular form of transport to and from the islands of the region.

Climates

The climates of South Asia fall into three primary categories. Most of Afghanistan, Pakistan, and northwest India are considered desert or semidesert. These areas also include sea coast, farmable land, and high mountains. However, they tend to be hot during the day and cold at night, with little rainfall during a typical year. The western coast of India, along with most of Bangladesh in the east, enjoys tropical climates. The weather is hot and humid, with lush vegetation fed by rainfall throughout the year. Most of India is considered subtropical, including its enormous Deccan Plateau. For much of the year, the weather is hot and wet. In the winter, there is much less rain, but the temperature is still pleasant. Northern Sri Lanka is subtropical, and the southern coast is warmer and wetter.

As one might expect, the range of temperatures in South Asia can be quite dramatic. Temperatures of 50–55 °C (120 °F and 130 °F) have been recorded in the tropical zones of India. Yet it is not unusual for the mercury to plummet below –35 °C (–30 °F) in the mountains, where the climate is more like a subpolar zone.

This nomadic camel train is travelling across the desert of Afghanistan.

MONSOON SEASON

More than one billion people in India, Bangladesh, Pakistan, and Sri Lanka depend on the farmers who work the land to put food on their tables. Those farmers, in turn, rely on the summer monsoons. Each year, the monsoons bring life-giving rain to the fields. But monsoons can be tricky. If too little rain falls, crop yields are small and food will be scarce. If the monsoons bring too much rain, crops and entire villages can be washed away.

This is a satellite image of a monsoon that hit Mumbai, India, in July 2005. →

Because of its varied landforms and closeness to the sea, South Asia has many distinct **microclimates**. For example, the Himalayas protect India from the cold winds of Central Asia. So even though the **Tropic of Cancer** cuts across India, the country's overall climate tends to be much closer to tropical than subtropical. The Himalayas also protect the countries of Bhutan and Nepal. The temperature in these nations can be quite cold, and many of their peaks have snow all year. But during the spring and summer, the melting ice on the slopes fills rivers and streams, making farming possible on lowlands and plateaus. The same is true in the Kashmir region of India and Pakistan.

← These two girls are travelling on a makeshift raft through the flooded village of Deochur in northeastern India in June 2005. Heavy monsoon rains caused severe flooding in the region.

People

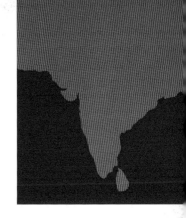

In most regions of the world, about half the people live in large towns and cities. In South Asia, only one person in five lives in an urban environment. The majority of people live in small villages. These populations generally rely on farming for most of their food, and some also earn a living making or assembling products that are shipped to other countries. There is often political unrest in the countryside, and sometimes food is scarce. These are some of the many reasons why people move to the region's cities. Young people also move to urban environments to find better education and job opportunities.

The cities of South Asia are busy and crowded. Many people struggle to survive, and quality housing for the poor is almost nonexistent. In some cases, entire families must share one room in an apartment block. Those who cannot afford basic housing must live in temporary structures on the outskirts of cities.

Despite these difficult conditions, the cities of South Asia continue to grow in physical size and population. This is because the economies of many countries in the region are doing very well, and more people have more money to spend. As these people look for homes in the middle of cities, those living on the fringes are pushed further out.

← Adam's Peak, also known as Sri Pada, in Sri Lanka is an important religious site for Buddhists, Hindus, Muslims, Jews, and Christians.

Growing cities

Better sanitation and health care, as well as advances in food-growing technology, have made it possible for people to live in more crowded spaces. If current trends continue, cities in South Asia will continue to grow larger and may one day connect with each other in **urban corridors**, where the edges of growing metropolitan areas meet each other. This has already occurred in countries on the **Pacific Rim**, such as Japan and China.

POPULATION EXPLOSION

The rich soil and warm weather of Bangladesh enable crops such as rice to be harvested three times a year. The availability of food is a major reason why the country's population rose from 30 million to more than 140 million in just over 100 years. Today, Bangladesh is one of the most densely populated countries in the world.

Religious life

Religious life is extremely important to the people of South Asia. For most people in this part of the world, religious authority is more important than political or **civil authority**. In some places the religious leadership and the government are the same thing. The religions of South Asia have made some of the region's greatest accomplishments possible, but they have also fuelled bitter fighting. Afghanistan, Pakistan, Bangladesh, and the Maldives are Islamic countries. In India and Nepal, most people follow the Hindu religion, although India also has large Muslim and Christian populations. In Bhutan and Sri Lanka, the main religion is Buddhism.

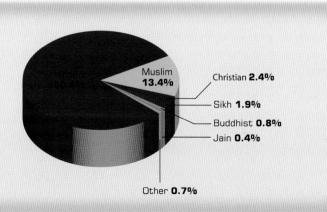

Muslim **13.4%**

Christian **2.4%**

Sikh **1.9%**

Buddhist **0.8%**

Jain **0.4%**

Other **0.7%**

◀ This chart shows the percentages of the Indian population that belong to various religions. India is the most religiously diverse country in South Asia.

People practice several other religions in South Asia. Although **Judaism** is not generally associated with South Asia, Jews have been living in India for more than 2,000 years. The first Jews in the region, known as the Cochin Jews, arrived in the city of Cochin about 2,500 years ago. Small, modern communities of Jews exist throughout the area.

Hinduism

Hinduism is older than any other organized religion, dating back to prehistoric times. Hinduism has no single founder or god that is worshipped, and followers are free to embrace new ideas. Hindus believe in a divine intelligence called Brahman, which runs through all living things. They also believe that all living things are part of a cycle of birth, death, and rebirth, called reincarnation. The goal of every Hindu is to rise to a level where one can break free of this cycle and achieve the ultimate level of existence.

There are more than 800 temples in the city of Palitana, India, a major centre for the Jain religion.

THE GOLDEN TEMPLE

The Golden Temple is built on one of the world's most peaceful and beautiful sites, in Amritsar, India. The temple sits on the middle of a sacred lake, fed by an underground spring. It is a unique mix of Hindu and Muslim architectural styles and is one of the holiest places for members of the Sikh religion.

There are approximately 19 million Sikhs in India. Their beliefs combine aspects of Hinduism and Islam. About 500 years ago, the Sikhs became a powerful force in the Punjab region of India, where millions continue to live today. In 2004 Manmohan Singh became India's first Sikh prime minister.

Islam

More than one billion people in the world are Muslim. They follow the teachings of the prophet Muhammad, who was born around the year 570. The word Islam means 'surrender to the will of Allah [God]'. The five pillars, or primary duties, of Islam are profession of faith; prayer five times a day; giving to the poor and to the **mosque**; fasting during the holy days of **Ramadan**; and at least one pilgrimage to the city of Mecca in Saudi Arabia. The Muslim rulers of the Mogul Empire controlled much of South Asia for three centuries. There are two main sects of Islam, Sunni and Shia. Although both groups follow the teachings of the prophet Muhammad, they disagree on important points in the religion's history and laws.

SUNNIS AND SHIAS

The separation of Sunni and Shia Muslims happened in the 7th century, following the death of the Prophet Muhammad. The split began as a disagreement over how the next caliph (leader) of the Muslim community should be chosen. One group believed the caliph should come from the Prophet Muhammad's family, namely his son-in-law, Ali. This group became the Shi'at Ali (party of Ali) and are now known as Shias. The Sunnis believed (and still believe) that power should not be hereditary and absolute, but earned.

Sunni Muslims tend to be more **secular** than Shia Muslims. The vast majority of Muslims who live in South Asia are Sunnis. Today, the differences between the two groups have grown and been exploited by outside powers, leading to conflicts in the Muslim world.

The beautiful Golden Temple at Amritsar, in India, is one of the most holy sites for members of the Sikh religion.

Government

The governments of South Asia range from kingdoms to democracies, but all have two things in common. Countries borrow much of their government structure from the European governments that once ruled over them. At the same time, they recognize that their traditions and beliefs have united their people over many hundreds of years. In the region's largest country, India, the people vote for representatives from different parties representing many different viewpoints and interests. The representatives debate important national issues, formulate new laws, and communicate their wishes to the country's leaders. India's political power rests primarily with its prime minister, not its president. The president's role in government is mostly ceremonial.

Pakistan's President Pervez Musharraf is an example of a South Asian leader whose power lies in his control of the armed forces. He seized control of the government in 1999.

Pakistan, India's neighbour, must balance religious, tribal, economic, and military affairs in a country of more than 160 million people – many of whom are poor and uneducated. Pakistan has been ruled by military leaders for much of its history.

Politics

The politics of South Asia are often extremely complex. In Afghanistan and Bangladesh, for instance, the struggle for control is between those who want a modern government that guarantees equality and freedom, and those who believe that the most prosperous path starts with a return to the fundamentals of Islam. There is an ongoing struggle in Sri Lanka, as well. Although Sri Lankans vote for their leaders, a minority **ethnic group** called the Tamils believe they are not represented fairly. They have fought the government for their independence since the 1980s.

Bhutan, one of the world's last kingdoms, announced in 2006 that its king, Jigme Singye Wangchuck, would step down to make way for a democratic government. Also in 2006, King Gyanendra of Nepal agreed to share power with an elected parliament. Maldives, once ruled by a sultan, became a republic in the 1950s. A republic is a form of government in which the people choose their leaders and lawmakers in elections. Maldives adopted a multiparty political system in 2005, meaning that the people could choose from candidates that hold opposing viewpoints.

YOUNG TIGERS

In many parts of the world where political groups are in armed conflict, children have become a common sight on the battlefield. One such place is Sri Lanka, where a rebel group calling themselves the Liberation Tigers of Tamil Eelam (Tamil Tigers) have been fighting the government for more than 30 years. They have long been accused of recruiting and sometimes abducting children to fight for their cause. The Tamil people want their own nation in the northeastern part of Sri Lanka. Realizing that they were losing sympathy and support from the outside world, the Tigers claim that they stopped recruiting children in 2003.

Although the Tamil Tigers claim that they no longer recruit and abduct child soldiers, many people do not believe the practice has stopped. Many people believe that children orphaned in the 2004 tsunami were quickly forced to become soldiers.

Culture

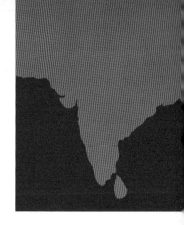

For thousands of years, people have been competing for land and resources in South Asia, and the result has been a blending of ethnic groups and religious beliefs. Still, the people of South Asia hold on to their national and regional identities. For example, Nepal is home to more than three dozen different ethnic groups. They may argue over their differences, but they all are proud to celebrate their common bond as Nepalese.

As technology has quickened the pace of modern life in South Asia, the pillars of religion and family are more important than ever. They provide stability in times of war, hunger, disease, and economic hardship – all of which exist in South Asia today. Unfortunately, holding on to the traditions of the past can also limit opportunities for women. In some countries, including Pakistan, most women have few rights and little or no access to education unless they are able to leave the country.

The greatest overall concern in the region is overpopulation. South Asia has taken great strides in food production, science and energy, and public health. Yet with the population growing by millions each year, the poorest people do not benefit from these advances as they should. The Indian government has tried with limited success to convince couples to have fewer children. In societies in which having large families has been both a matter of tradition and survival for centuries, it is very difficult to convince people to change their ways.

← Hindus bathe in the River Ganges in the holy city of Varanasi, India. Human waste is one of the many factors that contribute to the pollution of the sacred river.

THE CASTE SYSTEM

For many centuries, Hindu society has been divided into four social levels, or **castes**. At the top are the priests, or Brahmins. Next come the Kshatriyas, made up of nobility and military officers. Professionals and business people make up the third caste, called the Vaishyas, and servants and skilled labourers are called Sudras, the fourth caste. People outside the caste system used to be called untouchables. They are now called *harijans*, which means 'children of God'. Though more Hindus are marrying outside their caste, the practice is still unusual. In some parts of India, social interaction between members of different castes is still frowned upon. The relaxing of the caste system has begun in India's cities, but the system is still quite rigid in rural areas. The Indian government has outlawed the caste system, but many people believe it will always exist in Indian culture.

Culture in Afghanistan and Pakistan

The northwest region of South Asia includes the countries of Afghanistan and Pakistan. Afghanistan is almost three times the size of the United Kingdom. It is home to more than 30 million people. For much of its history, Afghanistan served as a gateway between China and India, and between the Middle East and Europe. The people controlling the mountain passages along these routes became rich and powerful. For many centuries, great kingdoms rose and fell. As more trade and travel took place by sea and by air, Afghanistan lost its importance and became one of the world's poorest countries. Years of military conflict also made life difficult for its people. To survive, many have turned to the three cultural influences that for centuries have taken them through good times and bad – herding, tribal and family connections, and their religious faith.

← These men have gathered for a meeting in their village near Mazar-i-Sharif in Afghanistan.

Tribal ties and religious life are important to the people of Pakistan. However, its cities, including Karachi and Lahore, are dynamic centres of commerce and education. Pakistan has become a world economic power, which has increased the quality of life for millions of its people. Many Pakistanis take their skills and experience abroad, finding opportunities in other countries. As Pakistan offers more opportunity and stability, its leaders hope to keep its most talented workers at home.

GETTING THE GOAT

Afghanistan is known for its exciting and dangerous national sport, Buzkashi. It is similar to polo and is played on horseback. Instead of a ball, players use the headless body of a goat. Points are scored by players who are able to break free from the pack and carry the goat over the end line, or toss it into a circle or special container. Buzkashi has been featured in movies starring Sylvester Stallone, Sean Connery, Tom Selleck, and Omar Sharif.

Eid-ul-Fitr

The spirit of Pakistan is truly on display during the Eid-ul-Fitr (Eid) festival, which marks the end of Ramadan. Families prepare for this celebration by buying colourful clothing and accessories, including glass bangles. They feast for two days as they break a month of daytime fasting in one gigantic party. Some people have compared the joyous feeling of Eid-ul-Fitr to the Christian holiday of Christmas. People exchange greetings of 'blessed Eid' or 'happy Eid', and adults are encouraged to give gifts to children.

The role of women in Afghanistan, and other South Asian countries, is often dependent on who is in charge. These refugee women are living in an abandoned building in Kabul.

Cultures of India

As in many parts of the world, family is everything to the people of India. In this vast nation (and in Sri Lanka, too), the importance of family is best expressed by the custom of keeping extended families – often with three or four generations – in one home, or at least in nearby houses or apartments. Because of this close-knit family structure, most important decisions are made by the adults in the house. Children are taught to respect and accept these decisions, and as they grow to adulthood, they continue to consult their elders on important decisions.

One area in which this is beginning to change, however, is marriage. The prearranged choice of a husband or wife for a child is a very old tradition in Indian families. Sometimes this arrangement is made when children are still young. Today, many young people are resisting arranged marriage and choosing their own partners.

Urban and rural

India has many large cities, but most people still live in villages. Far from the bright lights of places such as Mumbai and New Delhi, millions of Indians live, work, and dress as they have for generations. Their homes and businesses are simple, and running water and electricity are still considered luxuries in some areas.

A generation ago, it might have been difficult for an outsider to tell the difference between a typical city dweller and someone from a rural area. Today, the differences are enormous. While villagers maintain their old customs and dress, people living in the cities have begun to adopt Western culture. Films, music, and the Internet have had a great influence over the way young urban Indians talk, act, and dress.

Tribal structure

Traditional tribal structures are also important in South Asia. The different clans of the **Pashtuns**, for example, have played a major role in the region for hundreds of years. They live by a code of honour and conduct that predates their Islamic faith by several centuries. This code compels Pashtuns to open their homes to anyone seeking help. It also guides them to give automatic forgiveness to those who humbly admit that they have done wrong.

There are more than 40 million Pashtuns in South Asia, and another five million elsewhere in the world. Pashtun culture is centred in Afghanistan and Pakistan.

BOLLYWOOD

Many people outside India have come to know Indian culture through its cinema. India produces more films and sells more cinema tickets than any other country in the world. The centre of the film industry is Mumbai, which was formerly called Bombay. The film industry there has been nicknamed 'Bollywood', a combination of Bombay and Hollywood. Indian directors have been greatly influenced by Western film-makers. More recently, the stunning images and lavish musical performances in Indian films have begun to influence Western entertainment.

Exciting and colourful Bollywood films have made the film industry in India one of the largest in the world.

↑ This boy is playing in his village in the Chitwan district in Nepal. The children of Nepal are no different from children in other parts of the world.

Nepal and Bhutan

At the northern and eastern extremes of South Asia are two very small countries – Nepal and Bhutan – and a very large one, Bangladesh. Bangladesh is one of the most densely populated countries in the world. Nepal and Bhutan are located in the rugged, mountainous terrain between India and China's **Tibetan Plateau**. For many centuries, these nations were isolated from the outside world. Only in the past 30 years have Western tourists begun to explore them.

Visitors to Nepal are amazed to find how often its people celebrate religious and culture festivals. There are dozens each year. In Bhutan, many cultural celebrations take the form of *tsechus*, elaborate dances that celebrate important moments in Bhutanese history, as well as ancient Buddhist legends.

THE SHERPAS

Nepal's best known ethnic group is the Sherpa people, who farm and tend herds in the country's eastern mountains. They are famous for their mountaineering skills and their knowledge of the Himalayas. In 2003 two Sherpa guides raced each other to the top of Mount Everest. The most famous Sherpa was Tenzing Norgay, who climbed to the summit of Everest with Edmund Hillary in 1953. Today, the term *sherpa* is mistakenly used to describe all porters and guides in the Himalayas.

Bangladesh

In Bangladesh, one of the major events is Baishakhi, which celebrates the Bengali New Year. This festival takes place each April and coincides with a period of harvest. Bangladesh is an agricultural nation, so a good crop is cause for rejoicing. Many of the people in this nation of about 150 million stake their very survival on the farms of the River Ganges and its tributaries. Unfortunately, nature does not always cooperate. Fierce storms from the south can drive salt water from the Bay of Bengal up into the low-lying coastal regions. Many people drown during these floods, and crops and drinking water become contaminated.

The big breakup

In the years following World War II, Bangladesh was known as East Pakistan. It shared its national identity with West Pakistan, 1,600 kilometres (1,000 miles) away. The people of East Pakistan were unhappy with this arrangement. They felt that West Pakistan had too much political and economic power. In 1971 Bangladesh declared its independence. A terrible civil war followed, but with help from India, Bangladesh won its freedom. Since then, Pakistan and Bangladesh have been separate countries.

The Bodhnath Stupa shrine is the most recognizable part of the skyline in Kathmandu, Nepal.

Art

South Asian art and music have influenced world culture for centuries. First spread by traders and adventurers, the sights and sounds of this region can now be experienced on television and the Internet, and can be bought in shops and viewed in museums all over the world. The visual arts of South Asia are closely related to the non-visual arts, such as literature and music. All forms of art in the region are based on a common set of spiritual beliefs that has existed for centuries. These beliefs are expressed in different ways through painting, sculpture, architecture, literature, music, and dance. The artists of the region all share the same deep connection to the natural world.

The visual art of South Asia has always been a mix of different images and influences. The region began its own modern art tradition in the early 20th century, after Indian painter Rabindranath Tagore introduced daring elements of Western and modern art.

Music

The South Asian music scene is especially vibrant. The most recognizable instrument is probably the **sitar**, which has been the main instrument in Indian music for more than 500 years. Outside Asia, its distinctive sound has been utilized by music stars from the Beatles to Jay-Z.

In recent years, the driving drumbeat of **Bhangra** music has become extremely popular in American and European dance clubs. The Indian film industry's worldwide popularity has also helped expose the music of this region to a large and enthusiastic audience.

Meanwhile, exciting new sounds are being created in every corner of the region. Visitors to Nepal, for example, are usually impressed by the music scene in the city of Kathmandu, where the influences of 40 different ethnic groups can be heard in the local clubs and concert halls.

RAVI SHANKAR

The ambassador of South Asian music to the outside world is Ravi Shankar, master of the sitar. In the 1960s, he influenced the work of the great jazz musician John Coltrane and also taught George Harrison of the Beatles how to play the instrument. Shankar's influence can also be heard in the work of the Rolling Stones, the Grateful Dead, and legendary jazz trumpeter Miles Davis. Shankar's daughter Norah Jones is one of the most popular singer-songwriters in the world today.

↑ Traditional arts and crafts are still an important part of South Asian art.
This woman in Bhutan is weaving at her loom.

← These people are eating lunch at a restaurant in Bangladesh.

Food

The flavours of South Asia change with climate, geography, and culture. With a little knowledge of local agriculture and customs, a blindfolded person could probably guess his or her location simply by tasting the food. There is certainly no mistaking Sri Lankan cuisine – not only is it very spicy, but it combines many flavors that explode in your mouth. Sri Lanka has been famous for its spices for many centuries and was a favourite stopping place for ocean traders. Many of these traders ended up living in the country and introduced the cooking styles from their own native lands.

Spices

The South Asian spice trade played an important role in world history. Five hundred years ago, many spices were literally worth their weight in gold. The desire for exotic spices in the West helped launch an age of exploration. Today, the spice trade is still important to the region. India produces more than 45 percent of the world's spices. Nepal is also a major producer of spices.

CURRY ON!

No matter where one eats in South Asia, it is likely that curry will be on the menu. Curry includes a wide range of spicy, aromatic, sauce-based dishes. The ingredients in curry and curry powder differ somewhat from country to country and region to region. In Sri Lanka, where the word originated, curry often includes tamarind, coriander, ginger, garlic, cinnamon, cumin, and cardamom. In Bangladesh, mustard seeds and poppy seeds are common ingredients.

TEA TIME

Tea is consumed by every culture in South Asia. The taste and temperature may differ from place to place, but wherever it is served, tea is more than just a drink – it is often a reason to relax and socialise. Tea first came to the region from China, brought by traders travelling by caravan or ship. In the 19th century, English farmers began to grow tea in India. After the coffee crop was wiped out in Sri Lanka in the 1860s, the island became one of the world's most important tea producers.

Tea drinking is an important social tradition in cities such as Peshawar, Pakistan.

In northern India, Pakistan, and Afghanistan, grilling and barbecuing are popular ways to cook meat. These cooking styles were first introduced by Mogul rulers hundreds of years ago. In other regions of South Asia, meat is not on the menu at all for religious reasons. In Bangladesh, where most people live near water, fish is a major part of the diet. In areas where spices grow in abundance, such as southern India, foods tend to be spicy. In areas where spices are harder to obtain, such as the frontier regions bordering Central Asia, the food is milder. Almost every South Asian culture consumes either rice, bread, or both.

South Asian food is eaten around the world. In many countries, it is the most popular ethnic food. Each year, more and more people are able to try authentic South Asian food, thanks to companies that export regional spices and sauces. The city of Karachi, Pakistan, for example, is an important point of origin for these products.

Is the food you order in a restaurant the same as you might eat in its country of origin? The answer is yes ... and no. The food on Western menus is a blend of cuisines from different parts of a country. Often it is less spicy and probably contains a larger portion of meat than is typically used in a South Asian kitchen. Vegetarian cuisine in a Western restaurant, however, may actually be quite close to the dishes eaten by people in India.

Natural resources and economy

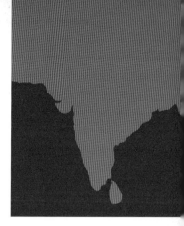

South Asia is rich in natural resources. Unfortunately, there are rarely enough resources to benefit everyone in the region's enormous, fast-growing population. New technologies have enabled countries to take better advantage of their agricultural, mineral, and energy resources, but the struggle to raise the overall standard of living continues nonetheless. In recent years, relief has come from the region's most abundant resource: people. In India and Pakistan, for instance, high-tech industry has become a major part of the economy. Of the many products exported from the region, the most important include a wide variety of textiles, rice, tea, spices, industrial machinery, chemicals, fertilizer, sporting goods, and gemstones.

The energy to run the region's businesses is supplied by **hydroelectricity** that is created from the streams and rivers running down from the mountains that ring South Asia. Nepal and Bhutan get almost all of their electricity from dams. India and Pakistan also rely greatly on this energy source. The Tarbela Dam, built on Pakistan's Indus River in the 1970s, is one of the largest structures of its kind.

← This cinnamon peeler works in a small village in Sri Lanka.

These factory employees are making computer printers on a production line in Bengaluru, India.

Precious resources

As the population in many South Asian countries grows, an ongoing debate rages over how best to use the region's resources. Is it better to sell them abroad or to use them to benefit the people of the nation directly? Bangladesh, for example, has large reserves of natural gas, much of which it sells to India. Critics say that the country's leaders should use the gas to create electricity and fertilizer, which would help the people of Bangladesh.

Agriculture

South Asia's exploding population makes the production of food a top priority. In areas where it is difficult to grow crops, such as desert and mountain regions, herding goats, sheep, and other animals is the primary source of food. Herding families get almost everything they need from their livestock – meat, milk, butter, cheese, hides, hair, and wool. What they do not use themselves can be sold or traded for other necessities. By contrast, people living in damp, warm regions, such as southern India, Sri Lanka, and Bangladesh, often grow their own food on small plots of land that yield two or three harvests a year. They depend on the rice crop and also include seafood in their diets.

The fertile Ganges Plain that covers much of northern India is the region's most important agricultural resource. There, a number of important crops are grown in huge quantities, particularly the numerous varieties of wheat needed to make bread. The Indus River valley in Pakistan is also a rich agricultural region.

AQUACULTURE

One encouraging source of food for the future is **aquaculture**. While millions of people in South Asia depend on the marine animals they catch with nets and hooks, millions more rarely get the benefits of this nutrient-rich food source. In Bangladesh, the brackish **delta** of the Ganges River has proved ideal for raising a species of fast-growing (and delicious) shrimp in vast underwater farms. This kind of aquaculture holds great promise for the people of South Asia.

These shrimp boats set up their nets in the Shibsha River in Bangladesh.

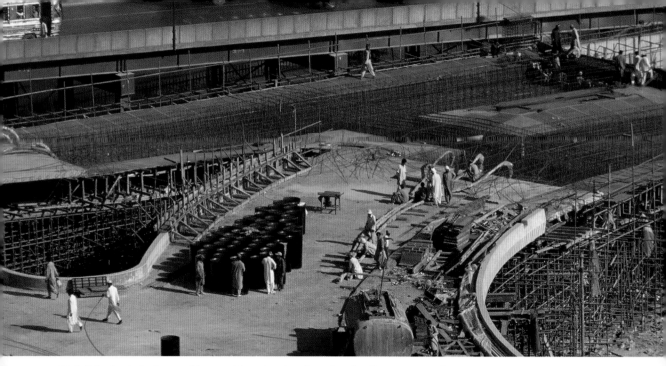

Pakistan has trained many of its most talented students in engineering. They are extremely important to the country's future. This new road is being built in Pakistan.

The economies of South Asia

The economies of South Asia vary greatly from country to country, but in general they lag behind most of the world. Hundreds of millions of people work in low-paid jobs or are part of the 'informal economy', providing basic services or performing simple tasks. Jobs in the informal economy include various types of manual labour, such as cooking, cleaning, or grounds maintenance, usually on a day-to-day or week-to-week basis. In some countries, three-quarters of the non-agricultural workforce is employed in this way. Of course, agriculture is tremendously important to the countries of South Asia. In India and Pakistan, for instance, it makes up about one-fifth of the economy. In Bangladesh, the production of jute, a plant used to make rope, is a cornerstone of the country's business.

The region's great economic success is India. The country has seen its economy grow many times over since it gained independence after World War II. India used its natural resources, such as iron ore and coal, to become one of the world's largest industrial nations by the late 1970s. The people were proud of this achievement but complained about the lack of consumer goods, such as cars and televisions. They blamed the government for its strict rules against foreign businesses setting up factories in India. In the 1990s, these rules were relaxed, and in no time, Indian shops were full of new products – and millions of new jobs were created by partnerships with overseas investors.

MAY I HELP YOU?

In many South Asian schools, students learn English as a second language. This is particularly true in India, where people have put their knowledge to work in the country's booming **service industries**. Many companies in Britain and the United States – including information technology, banking, and insurance companies – now route their telephone calls through Indian operators and customer service departments. This saves the companies millions of pounds because salaries are lower in India. It is also creating thousands of new jobs in India every week.

However, many people believe this system is not good in the long term either for India or for Britain and the United States. People worry that it could make India's economy too dependent on European and American companies, and prevent Indians from earning a fair wage. They also worry that it take jobs away from people in Britain and the United States.

Raising sheep has been done in Afghanistan in the same way for centuries.

Tourism

The many climates and cultures of South Asia, together with its ancient architectural wonders and great natural beauty, draw millions of tourists to the region each year. Where tourists go depends on how adventurous they are. The beaches of Sri Lanka and the Maldives are lovely, warm, and restful. Once seen, the rugged landscapes of Nepal, Pakistan, and Northern India are never forgotten.

All the countries of South Asia encourage tourism, some more successfully than others. Visitors are drawn in by the natural and cultural uniqueness of a region, and help its economy by spending money in hotels, shops, and restaurants. Tourism also promotes goodwill and understanding. All the countries in South Asia hope to share in the sharp rise in tourism to Asia as a whole. In wild areas, however, great care must be taken to limit the environmental impact of visitors.

India is by far the most popular country for tourism in South Asia. Its magnificent cities combine ancient and modern influences, and vibrate with cultural activity. The temples, shrines, and archaeological sites of India are especially popular with overseas visitors. Most sites are centuries old, and some rank among the most amazing and important structures on Earth. The most famous is the Taj Mahal, which took 20,000 workers about 20 years to build in the 1600s.

Other major tourist sites in India are the Palace of the Winds, Great Stupa shrine, Meenakshi Temple, and Gol Gumbaz mausoleum. Popular sites in other areas include the Bodhnath Stupa shrine in Nepal, and the tomb of Bibi Jawindi and the Imperial Mosque in Pakistan.

For those seeking more of a Western atmosphere, the Indian state of Goa retains the Latin flavour of the Portuguese who founded the city. Goa has one of the country's oldest established Christian populations, along with the country's best-known Catholic church. The state is most famous for its beautiful beaches.

TOP STOPS

Tourists spend more than £13 billion a year in India. Many tourists spend their time travelling in the triangle formed by the cities of Delhi, Agra (site of the Taj Mahal), and Jaipur. Organised tours to see the wildlife are increasingly popular. The country has nearly 500 protected parks and animal sanctuaries, 19 of which are part of the Project Tiger preservation programme. India is currently the third most popular destination for **adventure tourism**.

The Meenakshi Temple in the southern city of Madurai is one of India's most famous sites. Meenakshi is one of the few Hindu goddesses with a temple devoted to her.

Rich and poor

South Asia contains one of the world's fastest-growing economies – India – but also some of its poorest countries, including Nepal, Bhutan, Bangladesh, and Afghanistan. Workers throughout the region earn low wages, which makes it difficult for them to rise out of poverty. Many work in small factories, where clothes and other everyday products are assembled for sale overseas. The low cost of their labour enables their employers to sell the products they make at very competitive prices. Consumers in wealthy countries have become more aware of this situation, which affects a disproportionate number of women and children. As a result, some companies and individual consumers have begun to buy products only from companies that pay fair wages.

The Indian economy is among the largest in the world. Although two-thirds of its people earn their living in agriculture or a business related to agriculture, millions of others work in the manufacturing, textile, electronics, finance, and service industries.

On the other end of the spectrum is Afghanistan, which has been ravaged by violence for more than 25 years. There, life is a daily struggle for survival. Many people who have started businesses have no way to get their products to the outside world, and few in the country can

← In Nepal, children often work alongside their parents. However, children are also exploited as laborers in much of South Asia.

afford much more than the basic necessities. The farmers of Afghanistan grow wheat, rice, barley, and maize. In some areas, however, these crops cannot be grown. Some desperate farmers choose to grow poppies, which are used to make a dangerous drug called opium. Growing poppies may be the only way some farmers can make a living. As Afghanistan rebuilds, its leaders will have to make difficult decisions about how to deal with the drugs trade.

Living on less

There are many ways to judge how rich or poor a country is. One of the best is Purchasing Power Parity (PPP), which measures in U.S. dollars the value of the goods and services each person produces. Since people are paid directly or indirectly for what they produce, PPP can be used to compare living standards in different countries. The average person in the United States, for example, produces goods and services worth $41,000 a year. The top-producing country in South Asia is Sri Lanka, in which the average person produces just $4,300 in goods and services. The number for Afghanistan is $800. The purchasing power in other countries in South Asia falls between that of Sri Lanka and Afghanistan.

India's pharmaceutical industry provides jobs for thousands. This woman is working in a research and development centre in Mumbai.

Transport

The road systems of South Asia connect the major inland cities and also provide links to important ports. However, most roads except the major ones are still unpaved. People get from village to village however they can – by cars, buses, and bicycles, or in carts pulled by oxen, horses, or donkeys. Many people walk.

Paved roads are no longer unusual in the region's major cities, but they are often choked with traffic from a dozen different types of vehicle. In many places, people still travel by river, as they have for centuries. For long-distance travel, planes have become the most popular choice. There are airports and landing strips throughout South Asia. For those who cannot afford air travel, countries such as India and Sri Lanka have good railway systems.

Creating an Asian Highway system has been a dream of the United Nations since 1959. A modern roads system can boost the productivity of a country by 20 percent or more. This could lift millions of people out of poverty. Some progress was made during the 1960s, but the project has fallen far short of its original goal of 142,000 kilometres (88,234 miles). The Asian Highway idea has gained much-needed support in recent years, thanks to a treaty signed by 28 countries in the area.

Whether or not this project is completed, the countries of South Asia (togther with their neighbours) agree on the importance of creating a stronger **infrastructure**. The success of the European Union is due in part to the fact that goods can be transported from one end of Europe to the other on an unbroken network of modern roads. In South Asia, creating such as system will take more than mere road-building. It will involve developing energy resources and communications throughout the region, as well as improving the roads. Co-operation is the key. Banks must work together to finance these improvements, and governments must see themselves as partners instead of rivals, which is frequently the case.

THE KHYBER PASS

Although Afghanistan and Pakistan share a very long border, there are only a handful of roads that cut through the mountains dividing the two countries. The most famous is the Khyber Pass, which winds through the southeastern portion of the Hindu Kush Mountains. In some places, the Khyber Pass is less than 50 feet (15 metres) wide.

For more than a century, the easiest way to get from city to city in India has been by train. The trains are often very crowded.

THE MUJAHIDEEN

Because of the complex cultural and religious links that exist throughout South Asia, the impact of major events can be felt across many thousands of miles and many years. For example, during the 1980s Afghanistan became a rallying point for Muslims. The Soviet Union had seized control of the country's government, and a call went out to freedom fighters throughout the Islamic world to defend their Muslim brothers and sisters. These soldiers, called the Mujahideen, were able to repel the Soviet Union.

The Mujahideen were financed in part by the United States, which considered the Soviet Union an enemy. One of the most resourceful fighters was a young Saudi named Osama Bin Laden. He would later mastermind terrorist bombings at U.S. embassies in Africa, as well as the attacks of 11 September 2001 on New York's World Trade Center and the Pentagon in Washington, D.C.

Looking ahead

In South Asia, where millions of people live on the cutting edge of the future – and many millions more live as they did a century ago – the problems are many, and the answers are rarely simple. The leaders of these nations look for ways to encourage opportunity and prosperity for as many people as possible. Yet they also recognize that change can have unpredictable consequences. In an area of the world where military conflicts, religious bickering, poverty, and natural disasters are facts of everyday life, even the most carefully planned economic and humanitarian programmes can fail.

One issue that has come into sharp focus in South Asia is the treatment of children. Millions of children between the ages of 10 and 14 are expected to work to support their families. In many cases, this is because their parents cannot find work – often because they are uneducated or illiterate. By leaving school so early, these children face the same fate as their parents. Many organizations and government agencies are working to break this cycle. Addressing this issue is critical to South Asia's future.

As South Asia moves toward the second decade of the 21st century, the region faces a number of other complex challenges. In Afghanistan, no national government has existed since the 1970s. Politicians, warlords, tribal elders, and religious leaders will have to find a way to pull the country out of chaos. In Bangladesh, hard decisions must be made about the best use of the country's natural resources. In Sri Lanka, an educated and motivated population will continue to be held back until a solution is found to religious violence and civil strife.

India and Pakistan compete peacefully on the cricket field. This one-day international cricket match took place in Peshawar, Pakistan, in January 2006. Perhaps one day the countries' political relationship will be just as peaceful.

Complicating the future for this region is the fact that India and Pakistan – at odds for generations – each has nuclear weapons aimed at the other. Their quarrels are political, territorial, and spiritual, which does not make for a safe situation. Fortunately, with so much now at stake, the leaders of these two nations seem capable of looking beyond their passions. In 2006 the government of Pakistan indicated that it might be willing to negotiate peace in the long-disputed Kashmir region. This is the kind of development that makes the people of South Asia, and those around the world, believe that there is a bright future for this fascinating region.

Fact file

Countries of South Asia

Country	Population	Capital	Area in sq km (square miles)
Afghanistan	31,889,923	Kabul	647,500 (250,001)
Bangladesh	150,448,339	Dhaka	144,000 (55,598)
Bhutan	2,327,849	Thimphu	47,000 (18,146)
India	1,129,866,154	New Delhi	3,827,590 (1,269,345)
Nepal	28,901,790	Kathmandu	147,181 (56,826)
Pakistan	164,741,924	Islamabad	803,940 (310,402)
Republic of Maldives	369,031	Male	300 (115)
Sri Lanka	20,926,315	Colombo	65,610 (25,332)

The longest rivers in South Asia

Some of these rivers may start in countries outside the region.

River	Length in km (miles)
Indus	3,200 (1,988)
Brahmaputra	2,900 (1,800)
Ganges	2,510 (1,560)
Amu Darya	2,400 (1,500)

The highest mountains in South Asia

Mountain	Height in metres (feet)
Mount Everest	8,849 (29,035)
K2	8,611 (28,251)
KangChenjunga	8,586 (28,169)
Lhotse	8,516 (27,940)
Makalu	8,463 (27,766)
Chooyu	8,201 (26,906)
Dhaulagiri	8,167 (26,795)
Manaslu	8,163 (26,781)
Nanga Parbat	8,125 (26,657)
Annapurna 1	8,091 (26,545)

Timeline

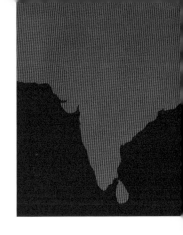

2500 BCE	The region's first civilization rises in the Indus River valley.
1500 BCE	The Aryans sweep into India, introducing the forerunner of Hinduism.
563 BCE	Prince Siddhartha Gautama, the founder of Buddhism, is born in Nepal.
711 CE	Islam is introduced to present-day Pakistan.
1153	Muslim seafarers bring Islam to the Maldive Islands.
1498	Portugal's Vasco da Gama explores the coast of India, beginning sea trade between South Asia and Europe.
1526	The Mogul Empire is established in India by Muslim rulers.
1576	The Bengal region (Bangladesh) becomes part of the Mogul Empire.
1757	Britain defeats Mogul and French armies in India to establish rule over much of the region.
1858	Britain officially declares India a British colony.
1893	Britain establishes the Durand Line, the border between Afghanistan and India.
1914	India sends the first of six million soldiers to fight on the side of the British in World War I.
1919	Afghanistan declares its independence from Britain.
1947	India gains full independence from Britain; the Muslim territories of East and West Pakistan are established.
1956	East and West Pakistan, separated by 1,600 kilometres (1,000 miles), become a single republic.
1965	The Maldives declare independence from Britain.

1971	East Pakistan declares its independence from West Pakistan and becomes Bangladesh.
1979	The Soviet Union invades Afghanistan; it withdraws in 1989.
1996	A religious group called the Taliban seizes control in Afghanistan.
1998	King Wangchuck of Bhutan promises to limit his power and hold free elections.
1999	India and Pakistan both conduct tests of nuclear missiles.
2001	Britain and the United States aid the forces of the Northern Alliance in ending the rule of the Taliban in Afghanistan.
2004	A powerful tsunami in December kills more than 50,000 people in South Asia.
2005	A bus service is established between Pakistani- and Indian-controlled cities in the disputed Kashmir region, reuniting families that had been separated for more than 50 years.
2006	Nepal's king hands power over to the country's new parliament.

Glossary

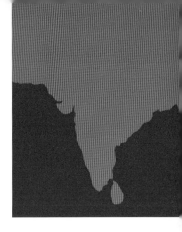

adventure tourism	type of travel that focuses on wild places
aquaculture	type of farming done in the water
arid	extremely dry
atoll	island formed by coral reefs
Buddhism	religion of Buddhists, based on the teachings of Buddha
Buddhist	one who follows the religion of Buddhism
Bhangra	traditional dance from the Punjab region of India
caste	social division in Hindu society
civil authority	system of rules that governs civilian affairs
civil disobedience	non-violent breaking of government rules in order to protest against their unfairness
colonial	from the era when European powers controlled countries in other parts of the world
commerce	large-scale buying and selling of goods, mainly between countries
delta	area that forms at the mouth of some rivers (usually fan-shaped) where silt is deposited and the river divides into branches
desert	very dry region with less than 25 millimetres (1 inch) of rainfall per year
dominion	self-governing territory
ethnic group	group defined by characteristics such as race, religious beliefs, or country of origin
global warming	increase in the average temperature of Earth's atmosphere, caused in part by burning fossil fuels and deforestation
Hindu	one who follows the religion of Hinduism

Hinduism	religion of Hindus. Hinduism involves a social system and the belief in a divine intelligence called Brahman.
hydroelectricity	electric power generated by flowing water
infrastructure	the basic services and systems, such as transport, water, and schools, that enable a society to function
Islamic	related to Islam, the religion of Muslims. Islam is based on the teachings of Muhammad and the Muslim holy book, the Koran.
Judaism	religion of Jews, based on the Torah and a belief in one God
low-pressure system	weather phenomenon associated with precipitation
metropolitan area	city and its surrounding communities
microclimate	small area with its own specific climate
monsoon	seasonal wind that brings heavy rain, especially in the Indian Ocean and South Asia
mosque	place of worship for followers of the Islamic faith
Muslim	one who follows the religion of Islam
Pacific Rim	countries that border the Pacific Ocean
Pashtun	tribe based mainly in the mountainous regions of Afghanistan and Pakistan
Ramadan	ninth month of the Muslim calendar, during which fasting occurs
secular	not pertaining to religion
service industry	any type of business that provides a service as opposed to goods
sitar	long-necked stringed instrument that originated in India
sultan	king or ruler, especially of a Muslim state
Tibetan Plateau	vast region of Southwest China
Tropic of Cancer	dividing line between the tropics and subtropics in the Northern Hemisphere
urban corridor	string of cities linked by shared roads and communications

Find out more

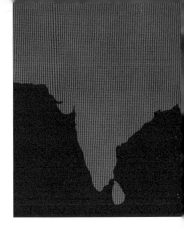

Further reading

Climbing Everest: Tales of Triumph and Tragedy on the World's Highest Mountain, Audrey Salkeld (National Geographic Books, 2003)
To The Top: The Story of Everest, Stephen Venables (Walker Books, 2004)
Indian Art & Culture, Jane Bingham (Heinemann Library, 2003)
Lonely Planet Guides, such as *Pakistan and the Karakoram Highway* and *South India* (Lonely Planet Publications)
Rough Guide: Sri Lanka, Gavin Thomas (Rough Guides, 2006)

Organizations and websites

www.cia.gov/cia/publications/factbook/index.html
CIA Factbook is the U.S. government's profiles of countries and territories around the world. The factbook contains information on geography, people, and politics.

www.grameen-info.org
Grameen Bank is an innovative development organization. The bank gives small business loans to poor, rural people in Bangladesh. Almost all of the recipients of the loans are women.

www.sawnet.org
South Asian Women's Network (SAWNET) is an online organization and forum about and for South Asian women.

Activities

Here are some topics to research if you want to find out more about South Asia:

Foreign investment
How does foreign investment help and hurt South Asia?

Global warming
What responsibility would world powers have if a country such as the Maldives were to become uninhabitable because of global warming?

Religion
How does religion affect the politics of South Asia?

Index

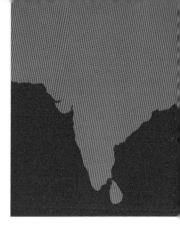